DATE DUE

1AY 3 0 2003		
APR 1 0 '06		
SEP 2 5 '07		

| Brodart Co. | Cat. # 55 137 001 | Printed in USA |

Giant Leaps

The Race to Space

Stuart A. Kallen

ABDO & Daughters
PUBLISHING

Published by Abdo & Daughters, 4940 Viking Dr., Suite 622, Edina, MN 55435.

Copyright ©1996 by Abdo Consulting Group, Inc., Pentagon Tower, P.O. Box 36036, Minneapolis, Minnesota 55435. International copyrights reserved in all countries. No part of this book may be reproduced in any form without written permission from the publisher. Printed in the United States.

Cover Photos by: Archive Photos, Bettmann
Inside Photos by:
Bettmann: pp. 4-5, 7, 9, 15, 17, 24, 25, 26, 27
Archive Photos: pp. 10, 11, 13, 19, 23, 28
AP/Wide World: p. 30

Edited by Bob Italia

Library of Congress Cataloging–in–Publication Data
Kallen, Stuart A., 1955—
    The race to space / Stuart A. Kallen.
        p. cm. — (Giant leaps)
    Includes bibliographical references and index.
    Summary: Describes the early efforts to develop space flight capabilities, focusing on the competition between the United States and the Soviet Union.
    ISBN 1-56239-564-5
    1. Artificial satellites, American—Juvenile literature. 2. Artificial satellites, Russian—Juvenile literature. 3. Space race—United States—History—Juvenile literature. 4. Space race-Soviet Union—History—Juvenile literature. [l. Space race. 2. Astronautics—History.] I. Title. II. Series.
    TL796.5.U5K35 1996
    629.4'09—dc20   95-38344
                                                                         CIP
                                                                          AC

CONTENTS

FLY ME TO

HUMAN BEINGS HAVE WALKED THE planet Earth for more than 100,000 years. They have been writing down historical events for almost 8,000. The Egyptians, the Mayans, and other cultures recorded the movement of the moon, the stars, and the planets with pinpoint accuracy. They celebrated the longest and shortest days of the year (the Solstices). They planted their crops in harmony with the planets' movements. And as long as people have been gazing at the stars, they have dreamt of flying among them. But dreams of space travel were just that—dreams. Humans were always caught in the steady pull of earth's gravity—that is, until October 4, 1957.

On that date, the Soviet Union's Communist government launched *Sputnik I*. It was a crude 184-pound (83.5-kilogram), unmanned satellite spacecraft that circled the earth once every 96 minutes. The era of space exploration was born.

Sputnik shocked America. It had been locked in a battle of ideas with the Communists for more than 12 years. There was an uneasy peace between two superpowers called a Cold War. Each side had thousands of nuclear missiles pointed towards the other—enough to destroy the planet 100 times over. If the Soviets could have an unseen satellite circling over our country, the Americans thought, what else might they try? Nuclear missiles from space? The small satellite circling the planet became a major cause for fear. Americans were sure *Sputnik* was spying on them. "How long would it be before Soviet soldiers were looking down on us?"

The Cold War was not just between the United States and the Soviet Union. Every country in the world was expected to choose sides. The two superpowers tried to show

This page: The Russian earth satellite *Sputnik* shown in one of the first official photos of the device.

THE MOON

the world that each was scientifically superior. Suddenly, *Sputnik* became a race to put a man on the moon. Americans felt they must be the first. U.S. Senator and later president Lyndon B. Johnson declared: "I, for one, don't want to go to bed by the light of a Communist moon." The new space age quickly became a space race.

The two most powerful countries on earth began to marshal their vast resources to put a human in space. It was politics. But it was more. It was the ancient human urge to explore the unknown. The Cold War provided the background—the urge to claim new territory, to occupy the moon, to colonize space. But the goals were the same for all explorers—to get there alive, to look around, to get home safely, and to tell the world.

When Christopher Columbus first sailed for the New World, he used the technology of the time— wooden ships, canvas sails, navigation instruments, and a few maps. But in the 1950s, space technology was only just being invented. The exploding rockets, the odd modules, and the computerized instruments were still on engineers' drawing boards. Columbus sailed with money borrowed from the King and Queen of Spain. American astronauts would need the help of thousands and thousands of people. In fact, it would take an entire nation with billions of dollars to get the job done. From factory workers to astrophysicists, America pulled together to compete with the Soviets. And it was a difficult task.

New communications technology allowed all Americans to take part in the space program. Moments before the first manned flight, trucks and cars pulled off the road to listen to the countdown on the radio. People lined up in front of TVs nervously watching the rockets fly into space. The astronauts' voices were beamed back from space to mission control and then out to a waiting world.

When *Sputnik* began its first orbit in the fall of 1957, it signaled a new age in space exploration. It led to one of the most thrilling events in human history—a man walking on the moon.

Right: The news that Russia had launched a "moon" got plenty of space in newspapers.

THE FIRST ROCKETMEN

The beauty of space flight had its beginnings in the horrors of war. On September 8, 1944, a high powered explosion rocked a London, England suburb called Chiswick. World War II was raging, and England had been taking hits from the Nazi bombers for more than three years. As the city burned, English bomb experts scratched their heads. There had been no airplane to deliver the bomb. The skies were clear. Radar had not detected any planes. How did the bomb get there?

The cause of the explosion in Chiswick was a German ballistic rocket named by the Nazis "Vengeance Weapon 2" or V-2. The bomb had been launched six minutes earlier from the Nazi-occupied Netherlands, over 100 miles (161 kilometers) away. It was fueled by alcohol and liquid oxygen, stood 46 feet (14.2 meters) high, and weighed 14 tons (12.6 metric tons). The nose was packed with a metric ton (2,204 pounds) of high explosives.

The V-2 had climbed into the air slowly and arched into a trajectory towards London. After 63 seconds, the rocket was 23 miles (37 kilometers) high and traveling at the speed of one mile (1.6 kilometers) per second. Automatic timers closed the valves on the propellant tanks over England. With no rocket power left, the bomb fell to earth traveling 2,000 miles (3,218 kilometers) per hour, faster than a rifle bullet. The thirteen people killed by the bomb were the first casualties of a space weapon. Over the next six months, 1,114 more V-2s fell on England killing almost 3,000 men, women, and children. Over 2,000 of the V-2s fell on Antwerp, Belgium. After World War II ended, Supreme Allied Commander General Dwight Eisenhower admitted that if the Nazis had invented the V-2 rocket sooner, the United States and its Allies might never have won the war.

Right: This is an actual launching of a German V-2 rocket at Peenem Ÿnde, the major Nazi guided missile research-and-testing center.

THE ROCKET PIONEER

The pioneer of rocket science was American Robert H. Goddard. Goddard worked in the early 20th century perfecting liquid-fuel rocket propulsion. In 1919 he wrote a book, *A Method of Reaching Extreme Altitudes*, in which he suggested that a rocket could reach the moon. Goddard launched the world's first liquid-fuel rocket from his aunt's Massachusetts cabbage patch in March 1926. The rocket used a mixture of gasoline and liquid oxygen. In 1929, Goddard sent up the first rocket to carry a barometer, a thermometer, and a small camera. From 1930 to 1942, Goddard worked in New Mexico building rockets that reached speeds of 550 miles (885 kilometers) per hour. They reached heights of 1.5 miles (2 kilometers). Goddard held 200 patents for rocket technology. During World War II, Goddard was director of research for the U.S. Navy. His work was mostly ignored during his lifetime. It was basic, however, to the V-2 weapons German rocket scientists developed.

The rockets that later took men to the moon were based on concepts, patents, and research done by Goddard.

Above: Dr. Robert H. Goddard in his rocket workshop.

Right: September 29, 1928. Goddard with rocket, showing combustion chamber and nozzle at the top of the framework. In this test, the rocket rose but caught at the top of the tower.

VON BRAUN'S ROCKETS

The V-2 had been designed and invented by a team of German engineers under the leadership of a young Prussian named Wernher von Braun. He was to become one of the giants of American space flight and become acting director of NASA in spite of his Nazi past.

Wernher von Braun was born in 1912 in East Prussia. When he was 18 he met Professor Hermann Oberth, a German who had written many papers on the use of rockets for interplanetary space flight. After reading Oberth's writings, von Braun believed that liquid-fueled rockets could one day be made large enough to carry humans to the moon and beyond. Von Braun began to spend time with other students launching tiny missiles in a weedy field outside Berlin. After a few years, they developed a crude rocket that burned liquid oxygen and gasoline. The rocket club was noticed one day by a general who was in charge of re-arming Germany after World War I. Rockets were still considered toys by the world. But the general urged von Braun to finish his education. In 1934, he received a Ph.D. in physics from the University of Berlin.

When the Nazis took power in Germany in 1933, von Braun's rocket team continued their research with a small budget. The Nazis moved von Braun into a rocket research center in 1937 in the village of PeenemŸnde on a peninsula of the Baltic Ocean in Germany. It was a major rocket laboratory that took over two years to build. But after the Nazis invaded Poland in 1939, von Braun's rocket team was ignored by Germany's leader, Adolph Hitler.

The team continued to grow however. They had to overcome problems of flight stability, fuel management, fuel pressure, engine cooling, and guidance. After a few successful launches, the Nazi command began to believe in von Braun's research. The country was scoured for rocket experts and funds were provided for expansion.

Right: As one of the Nazi's missile men, Wernher von Braun, in dark suit, helped construct the V-2 rocket.

By 1942 von Braun's team developed the A-4, which could carry a ton of explosives accurately to a target 180 miles (289.6 kilometers) away. When the first rocket went up, a general said to von Braun, "Today the spaceship was born!"

In 1943, Hitler decided that the A-4 rocket could help the Nazis win the war. He ordered the rocket into mass production. He also changed the name of the rocket from A-4 to "Vengeance Weapon 2." The Nazis forced thousands of concentration camp prisoners to build V-2 rockets in abandoned mine shafts near Nordhausen in the Harz mountains. The slave laborers were building 900 rockets per month. But at a terrible price. Over 150 workers died every day from starvation. And many workers purposely assembled the rockets wrong so they would not work. Those caught were shot.

Meanwhile, von Braun was designing multiple stage rockets that were truly monstrous. They could orbit a 30-ton (27.2-metric ton) payload.

By 1945, it was plain to von Braun that the Nazis were going to lose the war. He called a secret meeting with his staff and made plans to defect to the victors. His goal was to continue research to build rockets for human space travel. The team decided the United States would be the best country to offer their services to.

Wernher von Braun's team packed the entire PeenemŸnde archives, blueprints, test reports, and patents. They had enough documents to fill several boxcars on a train. They buried tons of documents in caves in the Harz mountains. Meanwhile, the Nazis planned on killing von Braun so that he would not defect.

On May 2, 1945, von Braun surrendered to American soldiers at a Bavarian ski resort. American teams rescued the buried documents and parts for 100 V-2 rockets. The materials were sent to the Army's White Sands Proving Grounds in New Mexico. While waiting to be sent to America, von Braun told the secrets of his rocket team's plans for multi-stage rockets to the moon and futuristic space stations. While the Americans did not take von Braun seriously, they let him continue experimenting with his rockets in the American desert.

Right: The tail assembly line in a V-2 factory in Germany during WWII.

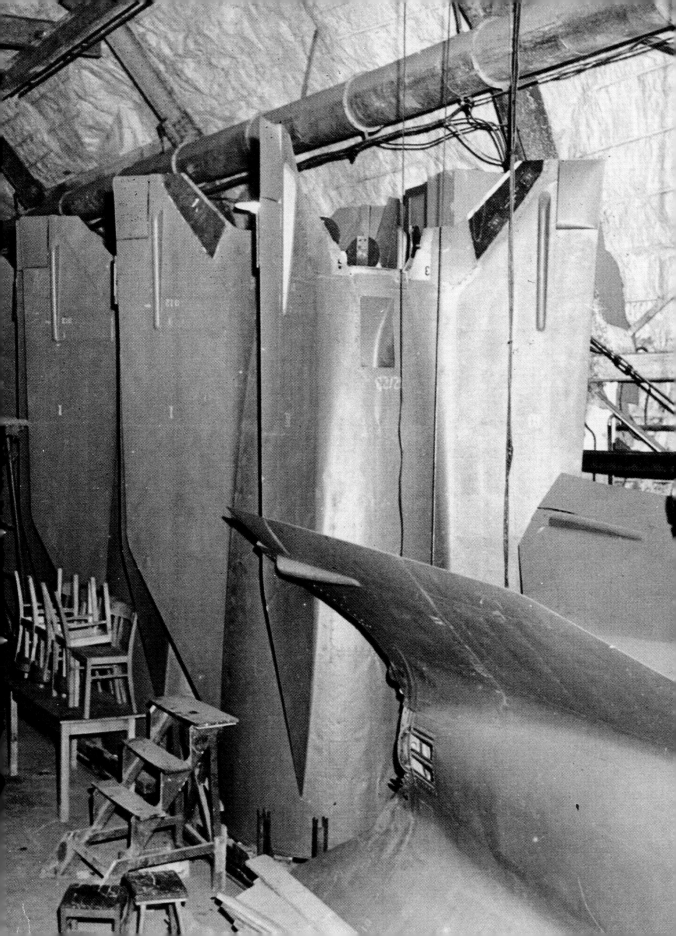

THE SOVIET MISSILE MEN

Besides von Braun, many German scientists came to America after the war. Almost as many went to work for the Soviets. While the Americans built bigger jet bombers, some of the men who had worked with von Braun helped the Soviets develop a rocket that could strike the U.S. from the Soviet Union. These were the world's first intercontinental ballistic missiles (ICBMs). While America ignored its skilled rocket team, the Soviets squeezed all the work they could out of their German scientists. On August 4, 1949, the Soviets exploded their first atom bomb. Now both superpowers had the Bomb.

The head of the Soviet rocket design team was Sergei Korolev. He had been inspired by Russian scientist Konstantin Tsiolkovsky, who had predicted the invention of multistage rockets, space stations, lunar bases, and permanent space colonies at the beginning of the twentieth century. Under Joseph Stalin's regime, Korolev had been arrested and held in a frigid Siberian prison camp for seven years. While prisoner, Korolev designed airplanes. When Stalin died in 1952, Korolev was freed and quickly became head of the Soviet rocket effort.

After Korolev learned all he could from the German scientists, he struck out on his own. He modified the V-2 rocket into the Soviet RD-107. Liquid oxygen and kerosene fueled the rocket, which had an amazing 225,000 pounds (101,925 kilograms) of thrust. Later versions had four strap-on boosters that fell away as the rocket rose. Korolev's inventions are still used, in a finer form, on Soviet rockets today.

Right: Sergei Pavlovich Korolev, Russian scientist and rocket designer.

MEANWHILE, BACK IN TEXAS

In 1947, frustrated Wernher von Braun was transferred to Fort Bliss in west Texas. Most of von Braun's rocket team had become American citizens, and their families joined them. Bored and in an alien culture, the German's kept in touch with their counterparts in the Soviet Union. This was strictly against the law.

Once the scientists accidentally bombed Mexico. On the night of May 28, 1947, a rocket team fired a V-2 from the White Sands Proving Ground north of El Paso. The missile veered off course and plunged toward the Rio Grande River. It exploded in a cemetery in Ciudad Juárez. No one was hurt in the accident but it did put the German rocket scientists into the public eye for a few days.

Von Braun spent his days putting together a proposal for an expedition to Mars. In 1948, eighteen U.S. publishing companies turned down the book, *Mars Project*, because it was "too fantastic." Once again, the public ignored von Braun's visions of human space travel.

After the Soviets exploded their first atom bomb in 1949, von Braun was transferred to Huntsville, Alabama, where he worked on the Redstone missile that would eventually put America into space.

Right: Part of the Army's Redstone Arsenal missile and rocket team. Beginning at top left, and left to right: Brigadier General H.N. Toftoy, Dr. Ernst Stuhlinger, Professor Hermann Oberth, Dr. Wernher von Braun, and Dr. Robert Lusser.

THE COLD WAR HEATS UP

By 1955, the Soviet Union had a new leader, Nikita Khrushchev. He wanted the entire world to know that Soviet technology was superior to America's. By 1957, he proved it when the Soviet Union demonstrated Korolev's ICBM. It was armed with a two-ton thermonuclear warhead and could travel 4,000 miles (6,436 kilometers), to strike at America's heartland. Korolev's rocket was also powerful enough to launch a satellite into outer space. Between 1955 and 1957 the Soviet scientists attended dozens of international scientific conventions. They told of their plans to launch a space satellite. Few people in the U.S. took them seriously. Soon the Soviets would surprise the world with *Sputnik I*.

As early as 1946, American scientists had plans for an earth satellite project. Using German concepts and studies, the newly created Rand Corporation worked with Douglas Aircraft Company to plan such a launch. The U.S. Army in the Pentagon rejected the plans as having no practical value.

In the mid-1950s, the Soviets were ready to launch a space satellite. U.S. President Eisenhower ordered the Pentagon to develop a space project. But it could not interfere with the Air Force's ICBM missile program. Working for the Army, von Braun promised that his Redstone rocket would place an American satellite in orbit no later than 1957.

The Navy had its own plan, called Project Vanguard. The proposed satellites would spy on the Soviet Union. The Navy and von Braun competed to design the best satellite rocket.

Meanwhile, von Braun went to work on a battlefield missile called the Jupiter, which was powered by the Redstone rocket. It would have a range of 2,000 miles (3,218 kilometers) and would have a nuclear nose cone that could survive the fiery temperatures of re-entry into the Earth's atmosphere. Von Braun secretly developed the Jupiter-C which could carry a 30-pound (13.5-kilogram) Earth satellite. The Navy suspected that von Braun would launch the world's first satellite "by accident" while testing the 4-stage Jupiter-C. That never happened. But on September 20, 1956, von Braun's Jupiter-C lifted off from Cape Canaveral in Florida. It delivered its payload to a South Pacific island 3,000 miles (4,827 kilometers) away. The fourth stage reached a speed of 16,000 miles (25,744 kilometers) per hour, just short of satellite launch speed.

Von Braun was ready to launch a satellite. But the Navy competed with the Vanguard Program. The Defense Department stuck with Vanguard even though its main booster rocket—the Viking—had major troubles. Defense Secretary Charles Wilson put an end to von Braun's long-range missile program.

Meanwhile in the Soviet Union, Korolev worked on an ICBM called the R-7. The missile had 20 thrust rockets and 12 steering rockets. When launched, it blew off 32 separate rocket plumes. The R-7 had a liftoff thrust of over one million pounds (453,000 kilograms), making it the most powerful booster in the world. After only two successful launches, Khrushchev bragged to the world that he could land warheads in America.

Korolev then received permission to launch a satellite. On the night of October 4, 1957, the countdown ended and the engines ignited. Plumes from the R-7's engines blasted the concrete launch pad. As the rocket climbed, its glare cast a huge shadow on the nearby base. The ground shook. Korolev watched the launch through a periscope and then turned on the radar to track the rocket's flight path. Radio receivers were tuned to the satellite's frequency. Within a minute of liftoff, they heard the steady beeping signal from the 182-pound (82.4-kilogram) sphere. *Sputnik* was in orbit. The Soviets had won the first leg of the space race.

JUPITER GETS THE NOD

The day after *Sputnik I*, world headlines trumpeted the news, "Soviets Win Race to Space." The Soviets had beaten the Americans. The next day, newspapers said that Soviet science was superior to the U.S. America's confidence in itself was badly shaken.

Politicians jumped into the fray. Senator Lyndon Johnson said *Sputnik* was a national emergency and called for a full use of America's resources to beat the Soviets. President Eisenhower downplayed the event. He called *Sputnik* "one small ball in the air." He refused to admit that the missile that launched *Sputnik* could also deliver a nuclear warhead.

The Soviets were far from launching nuclear weapons from space. But Americans did not know that, and the Soviets did not want them to know. The Soviets wanted Americans to fear them. *Sputnik* was a huge gamble for the Soviets. They launched it just days after the first successful flight of the R-7. In truth, most of the technology was left over from the German scientists. But the Soviet Union was a closed society. The U.S. had no way to know how advanced Soviet rocket science was.

The day *Sputnik* was launched, Wernher von Braun finally made a breakthrough to the American military. He said that the Navy's Atlas rocket was hopeless and that his Jupiter-C rocket could take on the Soviets. Von Braun said to the Army, "Turn us loose and let us do something. We can put up a satellite in sixty days." The generals gave him ninety.

One month after *Sputnik*, the Soviets orbited a much larger satellite called *Sputnik II* which weighed over 1,000 pounds (454 kilograms). *Sputnik II* carried a small dog named Laika. For seven days, Laika circled the earth. The heroic little dog died when her oxygen supply ran out. Americans saw Laika as a warm up for manned space flight.

Eisenhower and the Army could wait no longer. They prepared to launch two satellites as quickly as possible. For the next three months, von Braun and his team worked night and day to prepare the mission.

While von Braun prepared to launch *Explorer I*, the Navy continued to experiment with its Viking rockets. Over and over, the Vikings crashed and burned. America watched the failures on TV.

In the summer of 1958, President Eisenhower presented the United States Congress with the National Aeronautics and Space Act. The space agency NASA was born. Eisenhower insisted that NASA be completely separate from the Department of Defense. It was to be a civilian operation. But in secret, the military had, and has to this day, run some affairs at NASA. They use the space agency to launch military communications and spy satellites. Eisenhower signed the act to create NASA on July 29, 1958. NASA took over some test centers at Edwards Air Force Base in California, the test

Right: The U.S. Army's Jupiter-C rocket leaving the launch pad carrying the earth satellite, *Explorer II.*

range at Cape Canaveral, Florida, and built a new center in Maryland called the Goddard Space Flight Center. T. Keith Glennan was made director of the new space agency.

On January 31, 1958, von Braun's team of German scientists prepared to launch the satellite *Explorer I* from Cape Canaveral. The Jupiter-C rocket would carry *Explorer I* into space. At 10:48 PM, the *Explorer I* was launched. It climbed into the darkness of the Florida night. Two minutes later, an automatic timer separated the upper stages. For the next six minutes, the rocket coasted to 225 miles (362 kilometers) above the Atlantic Ocean. A cluster of small thruster jets maneuvered the rocket parallel to the ground. Soon the rocket's fourth stage was fired by a remote button from the ground. The motor ignited and *Explorer* reached orbital velocity—18,000 miles (28,962 kilometers) an hour.

Two hundred and fifty miles (402 kilometers) above West Africa, the tiny *Explorer* satellite glided out of the darkness into the sunlight. The satellite was the size of a milk bottle and weighed 10.5 pounds (5 kilograms). Soon the American listening station in California picked up the beeping signal from America's first satellite. The next morning Eisenhower calmly announced *Explorer's* success to the nation.

Above: This is history's first space traveler, Laika, a dog put into orbit by the Russians in 1957.

Right: The Jupiter-C missile in place on the launching pad.

PROJECT MANHIGH

The Soviets and the Americans continued launching rockets and missiles all the time. *Explorer III* quickly followed *Explorer II*. *Sputnik III* quickly followed *Sputnik II*. America's satellites were wonders of miniaturization and high-tech design. They were much lighter than the Soviets'. But when the Soviets put a 3,000-pound (1,361-kilogram) satellite into the air, it was obvious that they were preparing to send a human into space.

There were many questions to be answered before a human could enter space. What affect would the speeding rocket have on the human body? Could a person function in a tiny capsule without going mad? Could a good life-support system be built to protect someone from the extreme temperatures of outer space? What about solar radiation?

To answer these questions, lab animals were sent into space to test the conditions. In one experiment after another, animals such as dogs, mice, monkeys, rabbits, and frogs soared into space. A variety of plant and vegetable life accompanied them. But the quick up and down of most rockets did not expose the animals long enough to outer space. The space program needed better testing methods.

In 1957, the Air Force Project Manhigh used a high-altitude balloon to launch a human passenger in a pressurized capsule. The balloon soared over 100,000 feet (31,000 meters) above the earth's atmosphere. Project Manhigh continued for four years, testing the effects of high altitude on humans.

Above: A Redstone missile is gently lifted into a verticle position.

Right: The rocket that in 1961 boosted the first Vostok spaceship, piloted by Yuri Gagarin, in a round-the-earth orbit. The spaceship itself is in the top stage of the rocket.

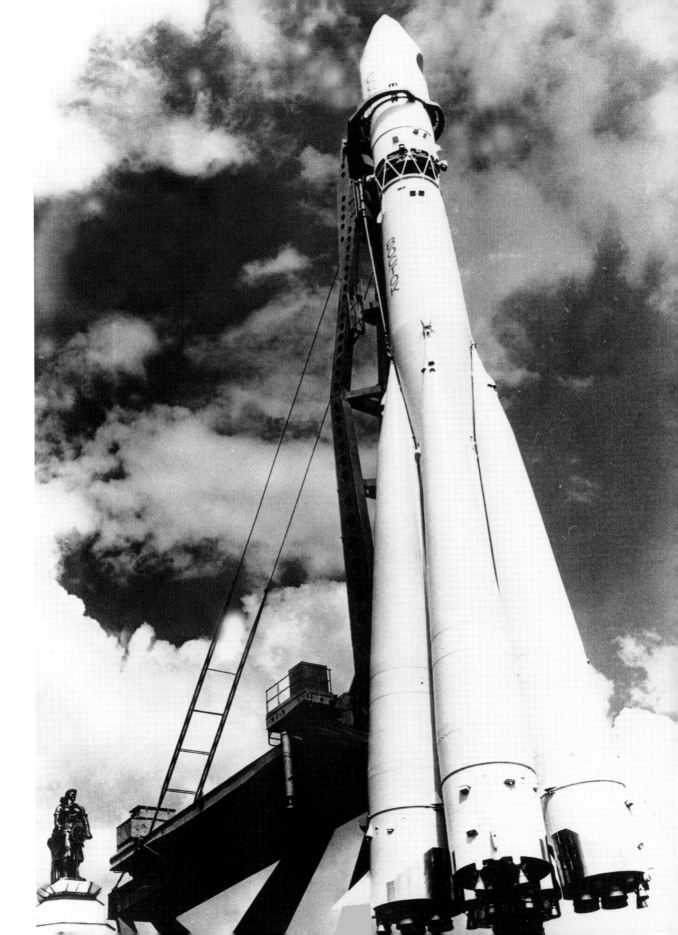

Above: Russian Cosmonaut Yuri Gagarin, first person in space aboard the *Vostok I*.

As the 1960s dawned, the era of unmanned space flight was coming to a close. On April 12, 1961, the Soviet Union put Cosmonaut Yuri Gagarin into space aboard the *Vostok I*. After orbiting the earth one time, Gagarin landed safely on Soviet soil.

In a few short years since the launching of the first satellite, a new era had begun. It was to be the most exciting—and sometimes tragic—period in space flight history. It would be the era of American astronauts, Soviet cosmonauts, and human space travel.

Humans were no longer bound to the earth. They had emerged from the atmosphere to gaze at the solar system. The restless human race could not stop now. They would return to the heavens again and again until one day, some of them would walk on the moon. From a crude rocket in a weedy field to *Explorer* and beyond, the human race had broken the bonds of gravity to which they had been chained since the beginning of time.

GLOSSARY

Allies
The United States, Canada, Great Britain, France, and other countries who fought on the same side against Germany and Japan in World War II.

atmosphere
The gaseous envelope surrounding the earth.

ballistic missile
A bomb that falls to earth using the force of gravity.

boosters
The first stage of a missile or rocket.

frequency
Radio signal.

intercontinental ballistic missiles (ICBM)
Ballistic missiles that can travel between continents.

interplanetary
Travel between planets.

orbit
The path of a satellite or spacecraft.

payload
What a missile carries, often a satellite or explosive warhead.

Peenem Ÿnde
A village on the coast of the Baltic Ocean in Germany where rockets could be launched over distances of 200 miles (322 kilometers).

periscope
An optical instrument that can see around objects with the use of mirrors and lenses.

propaganda
Ideas or news stories spread with the purpose of deceiving people.

propellant tanks
A tank that holds propellant—the liquid substance burnt in a rocket for the purposes of producing thrust.

radar
A device for determining the presence and location of an object by measuring the time for the echo of a radio wave to return from it and the direction from which it returns.

rocket plumes
Trail of smoke that burning fuel from a rocket leaves across the sky.

satellite
An object that orbits around a planet.

Sputnik
A man-made satellite launched by the Soviet Union, means *fellow traveler* in Russian.

steering rockets
Rockets that steer a missile by firing at specific times.

thrust
A force from an engine that propels a rocket, measured in pounds.

valve
A device for controlling the flow of a liquid.

velocity
Speed.

Dr. Robert H. Goddard in his rocket workshop.

BIBLIOGRAPHY

Aldrin, Buzz. *Men From Earth.* New York: Bantam Books, 1989.

Dolan, Edward F. *Famous Firsts in Space.* New York: Cobblehill Books, 1989.

Kennedy, Gregory P. *The First Men in Space.* New York: Chelsea House Publishers, 1991.

Olney, Ross Robert. *American in Space.* New York: Thomas Nelson, Inc., 1970.

Pogue, William R. *How Do You Go To The Bathroom In Space?* New York: Tom Doherty Books, 1985.

INDEX